D1603162

helices

GEORGE SWEDE

helices

ISBN 978-1-936848-70-6

Red Moon Press
PO Box 2461
Winchester VA
22604-1661 USA
www.redmoonpress.com

second printing

For Anita

Contents

Preface 9

Single Helix 13

Double Helix 49

Triple Helix 65

Beyond the Triple Helix 93

Acknowledgments 113

Recent Collections by the Author 120

Preface

All of the haiku, tanka and haibun in this book have been published since 2010 in periodicals and anthologies in Canada, Great Britain, Japan, the Netherlands and the United States. This is their first appearance in one of my collections

> traffic jam . . .
> juxtapositions jostle
> for the open lane

helices

A helix (pl: *helixes* or *helices*) is a type of smooth space curve, i.e. a curve in three-dimensional space. It has the property that the tangent line at any point makes a constant angle with a fixed line called the axis. Examples of helices are coil springs and the handrails of spiral staircases.

(*https://en.wikipedia.org/wiki/Helix*, accessed 12May2016)

Single Helix

sandcastle my carefully constructed self

the fantasy that is me central singularity

self-scrutiny
as deep
as the snorkel
allows

a grain of sand
in my umbilicus
the theory of everything

between what
I think and what is
lawn flamingo

tar pit an urge for immortality

all day writing poems . . .
the sound of paper settling
in the bin

snowdrifts . . .
i shovel the froth
from my latte

morning mist . . .
disconnected thoughts search
for conjunctions

my poems . . .
the woodcarver's
pile of chips

my bio —
the sun's glare thru
bare branches

papers neatly filed . . .
the smell of their gradual
irrelevance

The Puzzle

I'm trying to piece together my haiku
shards into whatever they were meant
to be.

> bagged leaves —
> notebook full
> to the last page

Green dots
filling the air among
bare branches —
a youthful longing
thought outgrown

Waiting for
the right light to photograph
the plum blossoms . . .
perhaps the right words
will come too

one more name
for the same ocean . . .
funeral notice

burial
a breeze from
my life cycle

Rhapsody

As the wind sways the tops of the trees,
a sudden urge to break free from the
gnarled knuckles and knees, the sunken
skin, the exposed blood vessels.

> in the camouflage
> of beached driftwood
> bones from the sea

waking with arms
across my chest — the coo
of mourning doves

window cobweb
a strand of my hair
not quite not there

Last night once more
I spoke before my mind
considered . . .
in the mouth of the black cat
a goldfinch still singing

My border guard
for thoughts without a visa
fell asleep . . .
the fugitive dream
slit by dawn's razor

one more day
with me in it —
skyscraper sundial

unsteady feet —
the increasing weight
of the past

Awake from a
dream of being lost
I gaze at stars
that might still
be there

A new day . . .
so much depends
on the angle
of light
in the mirror

Ouroboros

I am who I was meant to be. It is what it is. The universe is unfolding as it should. Such bromides make me feel better. The fact that they are tautologies doesn't matter.

> sunlit stone
> a snake asleep
> tail to mouth

What I want to say
censored by the time of
my tongue and fingers —
the dawn bird chorus
straight from the heart

Forces beyond control
made and now destroy me
bit-by-bit —
a second frost coming for
the last three lantana blooms

a small adjustment
to stay on route
sunlit pines

giant redwoods
my lungs recycling
their history

Bare bean poles
against the sunset —
a love song
from my teens
on the car radio

The towering gingko
we planted when knee-high
has lost all its leaves —
in time I will recall
whatever it was

thoughts at a trickle . . .
poking my pen
at the hangover

i try to give
the poem deeper meaning . . .
coffee cup flotsam

Inside-Out

The morning ritual begins — a blank paper, a pen and a latte. First to mar the pristine white are the starter ideas gathered during emerging consciousness: a faint scent of urine in an elderly neighbor's house and an odorous green pond.

> a bumblebee
> bumps the study window
> reflecting begonias

high wind
the forgotten parts
of our old house

desire
and old age —
the drip of the tap

how deeply should i
know myself — a large rock
on the well cover

earth's molten core i eat all of the apple

all the time
I've saved
nowhere to be
found

into the beyond
my thoughts lose
their hands

All the things
my shadow
has touched and
been touched by
I'll never know

storm ends words lie dislocated streets of air

White Elephant

I worry that an image from a violent novel might keep replaying because I don't want it to: swinging a child by the heels and crushing the head against a sea wall.

> low tide
> a baby bottle
> with note inside

for my age, healthy
the stone's last ripple
doesn't reach shore

20 below
the only movement
the 4th dimension

Another evening
with bare black branches
crisscrossing a sunset sky
and thoughts of what
lies beyond Sedra

In the bedside lamplight
a new topographic map
of my hands and arms
revealing even more
underground streams

Daze

Nothing's gone right this morning. Up too early. Body in passive resistance. Coffee not hot enough.

> after the long silence
> staccato buzzes from
> the window fly

Too many things that need to be done right away. Is it the wooden ladder that's unsteady or is it me? All our hinges are wearing out.

> shadows gone
> for months return
> one-by-one

glued
   by gravity to
4.54 billion years

i support
100 trillion microbes —
unfair tax hike

falling leaves
the growing lightness
of my bones

my shadow's head
on the other side of the chasm
a bank statement

only an eternal present jackhammer

at the edge of the universe a two-way mirror

starlight that left
at my birth, perhaps
in my eyes tonight

Long past
its perihelion
this life
overgrown
with dreams

In geometry, a double helix (plural *double helices*) is a pair of congruent geometrical helices with the same axis, differing by a translation along the axis.

In molecular biology, the term double helix re-fers to the structure formed by double-stranded molecules of nucleic acids such as DNA

(*https://en.wikipedia.org/wiki/Nucleic_acid_double_helix*, accessed 14May16)

Double Helix

wedding photo kiss
the merger of our
microbiomes

Sunday idleness . . .
from somewhere
in my DNA
a growl she finds
endearing

trees reveal
the coming storm
she undoes her hair

together at last the sounds of our prewords

first the stem then the leaves she and i

so gentle with me
her hands now cradle
brussels sprouts

Shocked awake
by a dream of being
cuckolded —
she's deeply asleep with
a Mona Lisa smile

Were there cries
of passion during
my creation?
In gray morning light
veins stand out

family squabbles
seedless watermelon
to end the barbecue

the wasp's face
what friendship
can become

Three best friends dead
before they reached sixty —
an ankle vein
pulses faster than my
watch's second hand

death bed watch
the fading sound of tires
on the country road

The Wait

He displays each "ess": weakness, unsteadiness, forgetfulness, tiredness, grumpiness — unsurprising in someone nearing 100.

when and how
the last crab apple
in its tree

a gravestone
with the name worn away
        gang tag

cemetery bees
her last diploma
made of marble

the river churning
thru the gorge — the son who chose
the wrong career

when understanding
starts then stops
birth cry

canyon campfire
our shadows as large as
the lives we wished for

fork in the trail
the overgrown path
gets long looks

Venn Circles

I'm bumping into things more even
though I'm shrinking.

    cemetery
    he now in the shadow
    of her

I search the obits
for once-good friends —
our garden's
daily births and deaths
unrecorded

coal dark tombstone
its eight numbers erased
by what they measured

Integers

One red leaf among
bare branches across
a steel-gray sky —
the last photo by the brother
who took an overdose

How do I know
did I really lock the door
what if I can't . . .
the back and forth pacing
of the caged leopard

I was in the life
of a famous person
who just died —
impossible to count
all the leaves on a tree

In geometry, a triple helix (plural *triple helices*) is a set of three congruent geometrical helices with the same axis, differing by a translation along the axis.

(https://en.wikipedia.org/wiki/Triple_helix, accessed 14May16)

Triple-stranded DNA is a DNA structure in which three oligonucleotides wind around each other and form a triple helix. In this structure, one strand binds to a B-form DNA double helix through Hoogsteen or reversed Hoogsteen hydrogen bonds.

(https://en.wikipedia.org/wiki/Triple-stranded_DNA, accessed 14May16)

Triple Helix

unnoticed in the flowerbed bomb's brain splatter

a monument
to a murderous dictator
mob of pigeons

Nazis shot father
and flung his body into
a mass grave —
wildflowers, butterflies, bees
on the memorial mound

mass grave site
a nesting partridge peers
thru the tall grass

Geology

The North African city's buildings resemble the fantastic shapes of weathered sandstone cliffs and ridges. Ordinary men have become soldiers during the revolution and fire rifles into the air to celebrate their freedom. Woman well-wisher on a twisted balcony is shot through the head.

the day's last birdsongs —
monoliths, buttes and hoodoos
in the graveyard

Nothing civil
about Cambodia's
internal war —
without a face
just one more skull

The garden flowers'
hidden roots in a struggle
for dominance —
a front page group photo
of smiling world leaders

Heat and Dust

The nation's leader chose the deaths of hundreds to save thousands. The famous poet wrote thousands to save hundreds,

rhino carcass stench the needs of old men

Sixty operations
to become a
lovely woman —
Cassini still
orbiting Saturn

The Mayan temple
under grass, shrubs, trees
for millenia —
one day scuba divers
will find Manhattan

Sentenced mass murderer
of a religious group
unrepentant —
out of the mist, then back
branchless, charred trunks

A public gang rape
of a young woman —
ants teeming over
a fallen fledgling
unable to get up

Pop hero has
five million followers
on Twitter —
the din of gannets
on the rocky islet

Dizzying doubts
about our perfectibility —
I find my bearings
in the hippocampus of
garden scents, droning bees

Feature obit:
90 years compressed into
a thousand words —
on YouTube a Porsche
crushed into a cube

gas station
the muscle car glows
with passed lives

Planned Obsolescence

Accused of war crimes, a nonagenarian is deported from Canada for trial in Hungary. He denies all charges and dies just before his court date.

> shopping list —
> striking an item
> no longer sold

the sprinter's shadow
does break
the world record

at last, the child's
violin practice ends . . .
mosquito whine

leaves before their fall . . .
a man on a park bench
studies stock prices

snowfall
the parking lot full
of bell curves

funeral service so many dying flowers

coffin display
the various prices
of absence

Much of what
is wrong with the world —
a crew digging-up
all the dandelions
from the huge lawn

first day of spring
ear buds everywhere
on nodding heads

fading into
oblivion's copyright
sidewalk cartoon

Warhol's 15 minutes . . .
so many pebbles
on the beach

a place in this world . . .
shells being ground to grains
by the rising tide

on a tour
of the half-sunk trawler
a school of dolphins

whale meat for sale . . .
the squeaky wheels
of the dolly

our need for attention —
the fish market's
many eyes

no-go zone
the twinkle of stars
in the Ukedo River

a wine-dark sea . . .
in the cruise ship library
no Homer

Time sculpting
my cohort into
distinct works —
a plop from under
the gala apple tree

The generation in charge
includes former students —
my field guides for
wildflowers, birds and trees
grown well-thumbed

Zanzibar
sculptures of slaves — tourists
with lengthening shadows

A snow cap
on the statue of
the dictator . . .
it tumbles from an
insurgence of air

refugee haven
the dead flies between
the double windows

freed for a while
the junkyard dog
lies on its chain

he hung his life
on a dead-end wall
crooked and faded
it finally fell
without provocation

whitecaps . . .
overboard ours would be
just two more

after defining haiku
each of us at our
own urinal

ocean sunset
the glow on the backs
of the selfie-takers

Night hurrying
down the mountainside
to work as shadows
for the day —
I re-knot my tie

Crowded subway —
the many selves
in each of us
at the windows
of our faces

Nucleic acid quadruplexes have been described as "structures in search of a function", as for many years there was minimal evidence pointing towards a biological role for these structures.

(*https://en.wikipedia.org/wiki/G-quadruplex*, accessed 12may16)

Beyond the Triple Helix

the day begins . . .
descendants of dinosaurs
darting, singing

bottomless, the well
of dreams — a chickadee
on the sill

living Fossil

A loved one asks for your attention,
forgetting your treasured twenty
minutes with a café au lait and a blank
page. You grow calm from the sound
and sight of the ginkgo leaves through
the blinds in your study.

> the living fossil
> flashes back
> the morning

The elm tree robin
grooming its red breast
in a sunrise beam —
the flow of endorphins
the eyes can trigger

It was just
expressing itself
the fence-top songbird
being carried away
in the cat's mouth

after i whistle
its song, the towhee
shows me how

waterfall roar . . .
the invisible line where
bird songs stop

What a trip to be you —
to climb my creation
to see it from all angles
to have it sustain me —
spider, wrapping your prey

abandoned cabin
flypaper sways
with its catch

geology chart
so many gnats caught in
the old cobweb

EXIT
four flies
in the cobweb

maggot-covered rat
white wiggly things
helped create me

below the sheen
of starlight on the pond
a food chain

Pisse au lit

The dandelion is one of nature's bountiful foods, edible from the florets to the roots. Moreover, it is rich in vitamins and minerals and can be used to make coffee, wine and salads. A minor drawback (or benefit, depending on one's needs) can be the diuretic effect of its roots, hence one of its other names. Yet their bright florets are seen as a scourge by those who have borrowed their ideas of beauty from the estates of the aristocracy.

neighbors in France
a galaxy of stars
on their prized lawn

wasteland
a pine recording
the history

small talk
the poplar and
the breeze

Fractals

Roots in good earth with a skyward trajectory and a branching out to engage in countless tropes with the sun and the wind . . .

century-old maple —
an ant in the still-moist
center of the stump

first falling leaves
vine tendrils sway too far from
what they could grasp

empty farmhouse
a vine wrapped around
the weathervane

Sunrise —
sketches of green
on the bare trees
in the hospice window
with the empty bed

During each lifespan
the many decisions
made by others —
crematorium smoke
over the cemetery

The Half-life of Memory

Last night's storm exposed bits of popcorn foam from crates unpacked in the backyard ten years ago — my share of mother's estate.

> trees in dawn mist . . .
> the diminishing shapes
> of the past

mid-winter
the stillness of the sardines
in the tin

Fish on ice —
whatever dreams
they had
gone from eyes
that cannot close

fresh pasture
the easy awkwardness
of cows

no sure answers
to life's questions
donkey hee-haw

dusk
shadows leaving
their bodies

ocean
the sound
of itself

Solace

Thoughts escape via fingers and tongue to what they imagine are freedom and fortune.

driftwood still wet —
the sea unseen beyond
the vast tidal flat

Acknowledgments

Front cover photo: The triple helical staircase inside the Convent of San Domingos de Bonaval Monastery, Santiago de Compostela, Galicia, Spain (from Pixabay accessed 14May16).

Back cover photo: Anita Krumins

Foreword: "traffic jam" *Off The Beaten Track: A Year In Haiku*, 2015

Single Helix: "sancastle" *Modern Haiku*, 2015, 46.2; "the fantasy" *Roadrunner*, 2013, 13:1; "self-scrutiny" *Roadrunner*, 2011, 11:2; "a grain of sand" *Bones*, 2014, No. 5; "between what" *Roadrunner*, 2013, 13.1 & *Haiku 2014* (Modern Haiku Press, 2014); "tar pit" *Rattle*, 2015, No. 47; "all day" *The Heron's Nest*, 2012, 14:1; "snowdrifts" *The Heron's Nest*, 2013, 15:2; "morning mist" *Modern Haiku*, 2013, 44.2; "my poems" *The Heron's Nest*, 2014, 16:1; "my bio" *Modern Haiku*, 2012, 43.1; "papers" *Modern Haiku*,

2011, 42.3; "The Puzzle" *Frogpond*, 2103, 36.3; "Green dots" *bottle rockets*, 2010, No. 23; "Waiting for" *Gusts*, 2010, No. 12 & *Take Five: Best Contemporary Tanka*, 2011, Vol. 3; "one more name" *Acorn*, 2012, #29; "burial" *Bones*, 2014, No. 5; "Rhapsody" *Modern Haiku*, 2012, 43.3; "waking" *Haiku Canada Review*, 2013, No. 7:2; "window cobweb" *Frogpond*, 2013, 36:3; "Last night" *Ribbons*, 2011, 7:4; "My border" *Ribbons*, 2015, 11:3; "one more day" *Modern Haiku*, 2012, 43.3; "unsteady" *Frogpond*, 2012, 35:3; "Awake from" *Simply Haiku*, 2010, 8:1; "A new day" *Ribbons*, 2010, 6:2 & *Whirligig*, 2012, 3:2; "Ouroboros" *Modern Haiku*, 2015, 46.3; "What I want" *Gusts*, 2014, No. 20; "Forces beyond" *Skylark*, 2014, 2:1; "a small adjustment" *Acorn*, 2012, No. 28; "giant redwoods" *A Hundred Gourds*, 2015, 4:4; "Bare bean" *Gusts*, 2013, No 18; "The towering" *Skylark*, 2014, 2:1; "thoughts at" *Acorn*, 2013, No. 30; "i try to" *Modern Haiku*, 2013, 44.1; "Inside-Out" *Frogpond*, 2012, 35.3; "high wind" *Haiku Canada Review*, 2013, 7:2; "desire" *Modern Haiku*, 2013, 44.1; "how deeply" *A Hundred Gourds*,

2014, 3:4; "earth's" *is/let*, March 29, 2015; "all the time" *Modern Haiku*, 2013, 44.2; "into the beyond" *Modern Haiku*, 2014, 45.1; "All the things" *Gusts*, 2010, No. 11 & *Take Five: Best Contemporary Tanka*, 2011, Vol. 3; "storm ends" *is/let*, 2015 March 29; "White Elephant" *Frogpond*, 2015, 38:1; "for my age" *Acorn*, 2015, #35; "20 below" *Whirligig*, 2012, 3:2; "Another evening" *Simply Haiku*, 2010, 8:1; "In the bedside" *Simply Haiku*, 2010, 8:1; "Daze" *Modern Haiku*, 2012, 43.2; "glued" *Modern Haiku*, 42:2, 2011; "i support" *Modern Haiku*, 2013, 44.3; "falling leaves" *Frogpond*, 2014, 37:1; "my shadow's" *Roadrunner*, 2012, 12.1 (Scorpion Prize); "only an" *Rattle*, 2015, No. 47; "at the edge" *Roadrunner*, 2012, 12:2; "starlight" *Fropond*, 2012, 35:3; "Long past" *Ribbons*, 2011, 7:4 & *Imaginarium 2012: The Best Canadian Speculative Writing*.

Double Helix: "wedding" *Haiku Canada Review*, 2015, 9:2; "Sunday" *Gusts*, 2012, No. 16; "trees reveal" *muttering thunder*, 2015, Vol. 2; "together" *A Hundred Gourds*, 2015, 4:4; "first the stem" *Haiku*

Canada Review, 2015, 9:2; "so gentle" *Modern Haiku*, 2013, 44.2; "Shocked" *Magnapoets*, 2011, No. 7; "Were there" *Gusts*, 2013, No.17; "family" *Modern Haiku*, 2012, 43:2; "the wasp's" *Rattle*, 2015, No. 47; "Three best" *Ribbons*, 2014, 10.3; "death bed watch" *Frogpond*, 2012, 35:2; "The Wait" *Frogpond*, 2013, 36.3; "a gravestone" *Modern Haiku*, 2011, 42.2; "cemetery bees" *The Heron's Nest*, 2011, 13:4; "the river" *The Heron's Nest*, 2013, 15:3; "when understanding" *Haiku Canada Review*, 2012, 6:1; "canyon campfire" *Muttering Thunder*, 2014, Vol. 1 & *Big Data: The Red Moon Anthology of English-Language Haiku* (Red Moon Press, 2014); "fork" *Haiku Canada Review*, 2013, 7:2; "Venn Circles" *Frogpond*, 2014, 37:3; "I search" *Gusts*, 2014, No. 20; "coal dark" *Roadrunner*, 2011, 11:2 & *Imaginariium 2012: The Best Canadian Speculative Writing*; "Integers" *Ribbons*, 2016, 11:1.

Triple Helix: "unnoticed" *Roadrunner*, 2011, 11:1; "a monument" *Modern Haiku*, 2015, 46:2; "Nazis" *Ribbons*, 2015, 11:2; "mass grave" *Muttering*

Thunder, 2014, Vol. 1; "Geology" *Haiku Canada Review*, 2012, 6.2; "Nothing civil" *A Hundred Gourds*, 2015, 4:3; "The garden" *Gusts*, 2014, No. 20; "Heat and Dust" *Modern Haiku*, 2014, 45:3; "Sixty" *Skylark*, 2014, 2:2; "The Mayan" *Skylark*, 2014, 2:2; "Sentenced" & "A public" & "Pop hero" & "Dizzying" *Ribbons*, 2014, 10:1; "Feature" *A Hundred Gourds*, 2015, 4:2; "gas station" *Bones*, 2015, #7; "Planned Obsolescence" *Frogpond*, 2014, 37.1; "the sprinter's" *Modern Haiku*, 2010, 41.3; "at last" *Haiku Canada Review*, 2013, 7:1; "leaves before" *Modern Haiku*, 2912, 43.1; "snowfall" *Modern Haiku*, 2014, 45.2; "funeral" & "coffin" *Frogpond*, 2015, 38:3; "Much of what" *Gusts*, 2012, No. 15; "first day" *Frogpond*, 2013, 36:2; "fading" *Haiku Canada Review*, 2014, 8:1; "Warhol's" *Haiku Canada Review*, 2012, 6:2; "a place in" *The Heron's Nest*, 2012, 14:3; "on a tour" *Frogpond*, 2012, 35:3; "whale" *Modern Haiku*, 2013, 44:1; "our need" *Modern Haiku*, 2014, 45.2; "no-go" Grand Prize, Kusamakura International Haiku Competition, 2011; "a wine-dark" *Haiku Canada Review*, 2015, 9:1; "Time" & "The generation" *A*

World Rediscovered: An Anthology of Contemporary Verse, 2012; "Zanzibar" *Haiku Canada Review*, 2015, 9:1; "A snow cap" *American Tanka*, 2012, No. 21 & *One Man's Maple Moon: 66 Selected English-Chinese Bilingual Tanka*, 2014, Vol. 1; "refugee" *A Hundred Gourds*, 2016, 5:1; "freed" *Modern Haiku*, 2015, 46.1; "he hung" *NOON*, 2016, No. 11; "whitecaps" *Haiku Canada Review*, 2015, 9:1; "after defining" *Modern Haiku*, 42.1 & *Carving Darkness: Red Moon Anthology of English-Language Haiku* (Red Moon Press, 2011; "ocean sunset" *Modern Haiku*, 2015, 46.3; "Night" *Rattle*, 2015, No. 47; "Crowded" *A Hundred Gourds*, 2015, 4:2.

Beyond the Triple Helix: "the day" *The Heron's Nest*, 2010, 12:4; "bottomless" *Haiku Canada Review*, 2011, 5:2; "Living Fossil" *Contemporary Haibun Online*, Fall 2011 — as Jay Marsh; "The elm" *Gusts*, 2013, No. 18; "It was" *Ribbons*, 2010, 6:2; "after i" *Acorn*, 2011, No. 27; "waterfall" *Frogpond*, 2013, 36:3; "What a" *A Hundred Gourds*, 2014, 3:4; "abandoned" & "geology" *Haiku Canada Review*,

2016, 10:1; "EXIT" *Frogpond*, 2015, 38:1; "maggot" *Sharing the Sun: HSA Anthology*, 2011; "below" *The Heron's Nest*, 2013, 15:4; "Pisse au Lit" *Frogpond*, 2012, 35:2; "wasteland" *Modern Haiku*, 2011, 42:1; "small talk" *Acorn*, 2014, No. 33; "Fractals" *Frogpond*, 2015, 38:3; "first falling" *The Heron's Nest*, 2013, 15:3; "empty" *The Heron's Nest*, 2010, 12:4; "Sunrise" *A Hundred Gourds*, 2015, 4:4; "During" *A Hundred Gourds*, 2015, 4:2; "The Half-Llife" *Modern Haiku*, 2014, 45.1; "mid-winter" *The Heron's Nest*, 2012, 14:1; "Fish" *Gusts*, 2012, No. 16; "fresh" *Acorn*, 2015, No. 34; "no sure" *Modern Haiku*, 2010, 41.2; "dusk" *Bones*, 2015, #8 & *Fire in the Treetops: HNA Anthology*, 2015; "ocean" *Upstate Dim Sum*, 2010/I & *Evolution: Red Moon Anthology of English-language Haiku* (Red Moon Press, 2010); "Solace" *Frogpond*, 2014, 37:2.

Recent poetry collections
by George Swede

Almost Unseen: Selected Haiku of George Swede. Decatur, IL: Brooks Books, 2000 (a Goodrich Haiku Master Edition)

First Light, First Shadows. Liverpool, GBR: Snapshot Press, 2006 (First Prize Snapshot Press Tanka Collection Competition)

Joy In Me Still (haiku). Edmonton, AB: Inkling Press, 2010 (ed. E.D. Blodgett)

White Thoughts, Blue Mind (tanka). Edmonton, AB: Inkling Press, 2010 (ed. E.D. Blodgett)

embryo: eye poems. Toronto: Inšpress, 2013

Le Haïku Moderne En Anglais. Rosny-sous-Bois, France: Éditions unicité, 2013 (trans. Daniel Py)

micro haiku: three to nine syllables. Toronto: Inšpress, 2014

Made in the USA
Middletown, DE
20 April 2019